essential
English
Starters 2
Pupils' Book

Louis Fidge

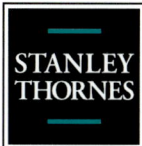

STANLEY
THORNES

Acknowledgements

The author and publishers wish to thank the following for permission to use copyright material.

Excerpt from 'Mandy likes Mud' by Gareth Owen from *Song of the City*, HarperCollins Publishers.

'I had no friends at all' by John Kitching, from *A Very First Poetry Book*, Oxford University Press.

'Row, row, row your boat' by Lucy Coats from *First Rhymes*, Orchard Press.

Excerpt from 'Helping' by Lucy Coats from *First Rhymes*, Orchard Press.

First published in 1997 by
Stanley Thornes Publishers Ltd
Ellenborough House
Wellington Street
Cheltenham
GL50 1YW

97 98 99 00 01 / 10 9 8 7 6 5 4 3 2 1

A catalogue record for this book is available from the British Library

ISBN 0-7487-2945-3
Also sold in the following packs:
Pack of 8 0-7487-2948-8, Pack of 16 0-7487-2950-X

Designed by Oxprint Design, Oxford. Illustrations by Debbie Clarke.

Printed and bound in Hong Kong

CONTENTS

Mandy likes the mud

Polly likes to play with toys
Melissa makes a lot of noise
Ann has a bike
Trevor has a trike
But Mandy likes the mud.

From 'Song of the City' by Gareth Owen

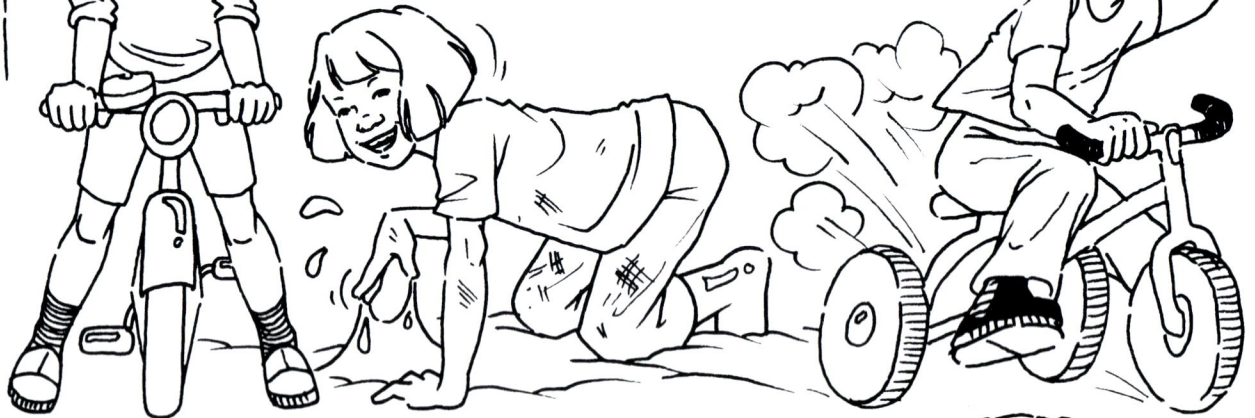

Answer these questions in your book.

1 Who likes to play with toys?

2 Who makes a lot of noise?

3 Who has a bike?

4 Who has a trike?

5 Who likes mud?

● Names of things ●

hat   sock   hill   net   sun

*Write the **name** of each picture in your book.*

1
2
3
4
5

Copy these word lists in your book. Join up the words that **rhyme**.

hat	rock
sock	bun
hill	pet
net	cat
sun	pill

> 'Naming' words are called **nouns**.

Make up some sentences using each pair of words.
Do it like this:

> *I sat on a <u>rock</u> and put on my <u>sock</u>.*

● Silly sentences ●

sea

clown

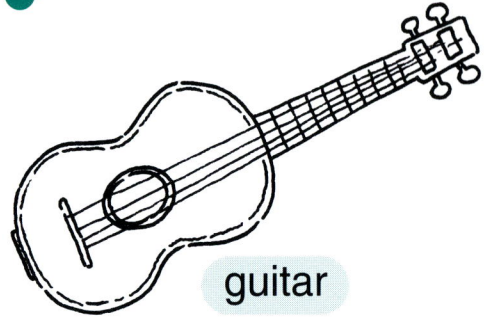

guitar

apple

book

chair

One word in each of these sentences does not make sense.

Write out each sentence correctly in your book.

The first one has been done for you.

1 The man was playing a ~~banana.~~
   The man was playing a guitar.

2 I like to read a bike.

3 The girl went for a swim in the door.

4 I ate my jumper.

5 A car has four legs.

6 The wall made me laugh.

Snakes and ladders

Some of the instructions for playing this game are missing!

Write out the rules for the game in your book.

Use the words in this box to help you.

> first   snake   up   hundred
>   six   winner   down

RULES

You will need a dice and some counters.

The person who throws a _____ goes _____ .

If you land on a ladder you go _____ .

If you land on a _____ you go _____ .

The first person to reach a _____ is the _____ .

Which games do you like playing? Make a list of some.

What the giant had for dinner

Match the sentences to the pictures.

Write them in the correct order in your book.

Then he ate a house near me.

First he ate a hive of bees.

Last of all he drank the sea.

Next he ate some chestnut trees.

'What the giant had for dinner' by Ian McMillan and Martyn Wiley

● Lists ●

I have got the same as you! Let's share them together.

cake

sweet

biscuit

banana

roll

apple

*Write a **list** like this in your book:*

Together we have two rolls, two _____ , two _____ ,

two _____ , two _____ and two _____ .

Copy this shopping list in your book.

Write the name of:

1 something you can get in a tin

2 something you can get in a packet

3 something you can get in a bag

Shopping list

1 _____

2 _____

3 _____

● Spaces between words ●

Tom and Tara talk very quickly! What are they saying?

Ilikechips.

Ilikebeans.

Write these sentences in your book.

Leave a space between each word.

1 Ihadcurryfordinner.

2 Ilikedmydrinkofmilk.

3 Iateapizza.

4 Iateacheeseroll.

5 Icanmakeacake.

6 Icancookeggs.

● The giant's week ●

Copy and finish the sentences about what the giant ate.

On Monday the giant ate a hundred eggs.

One Tuesday he drank fifty milk shakes.

On Wednesday he ate _____ .

On _____

On _____

On _____

On _____ the giant went POP!

Keep a food diary for a week.
Write down what you eat each day.

Friends

● The lion and the mouse ●

One day the lion was hungry so he went to hunt for something to eat.

The lion got caught in a net. He could not get out. He roared loudly.

A little mouse heard him. She bit the ropes of the net until the lion could get away.

The lion thanked the mouse. They soon became good friends.

Write down if you think these sentences are 'true' *or* 'false'.

1 The lion went for a drink.

2 The lion was caught in a net.

3 A rat helped the lion to get free.

4 The lion and the mouse became friends.

● Word families ●

Copy these sets of words in your book.

*Ring the pairs of words from the **same family** in each set.*

The first one has been done for you.

1 hum   (can)   mop   (fan)
2 jet   pip   gum   pet
3 bed   fig   wig   sad
4 dot   bet   pit   pot
5 rag   mug   jug   cog

Can you think of any more words from the same families?

Now sort the words above into different sets.

*Look carefully at the **vowels** in the middle of each word.*

Do it in your book like this:

a	e	i	o	u
can				
fan				
sad				
rag				

● Friends ●

I had no friends at all
Until you came my way
And now we play and play
All day. I only hope
You never have to go away.
It would be sad
To lose the only friend
I've ever really had.

'I had no friends at all' by John Kitching.

Write a poem about a friend.

Do it in your best writing.

Do it in sentences like this:

    My friend always plays with me.
    My friend never calls me names.
    My friend ...

Remember to check your spellings too.

When you have finished your poem read it and make sure you have put in capital letters at the beginning of each sentence and full stops at the end of each sentence.

● About me ●

My hair is straight.

My hair is curly.

I'm tall.

I'm small.

I'm friendly.

I'm shy.

My eyes are blue.

My eyes are brown.

*What are **you** like?*

Write some sentences about yourself.

Write about:

1 what you look like

2 what you are good at

3 what you like to do.

Books

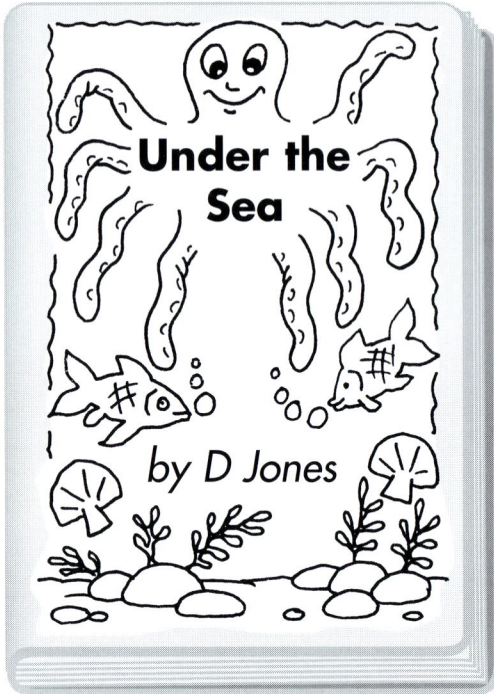

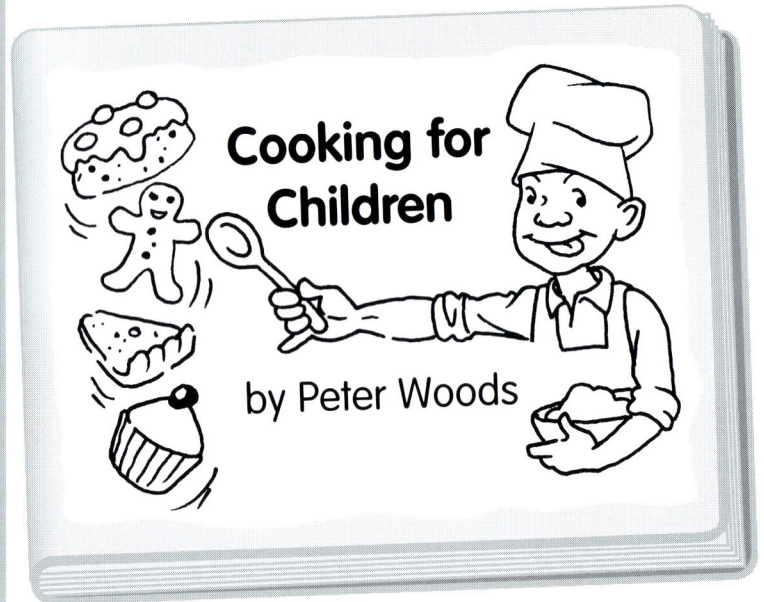

Look at these book covers.

Answer these questions in your book.

1 Which book would you use to find out

a) what you need to make a cake?

b) what a shark eats?

c) what a jellyfish looks like?

d) how to cook eggs?

2 Who wrote the book called

a) Cooking for Children?

b) Under the Sea?

● Dictionaries ●

Look at the first letter of these words. They are written in **alphabetical order**.

apple   bus   crocodile

Write these sets of words in alphabetical order in your book.

1 egg   dog   fish

2 net   lake   mouse

3 tin   rug   sun

A **dictionary** is a book that gives you the **meaning** of words. The words in a dictionary are written in **alphabetical order**.

Write what each of the words means. Do it like this.

Rr roof

Every house has a roof.
A roof is used to protect people from the weather.

Ss sandwich _____

_____

_____

Tt television _____

_____

_____

● People's names ●

Write the names of these characters in your book.

Use a capital letter at the start of each person's name.

snow white

hansel and gretel

father christmas

goldilocks

jack and jill

little red riding hood

Copy these sentences into your book.

Put in capital letters and full stops.

1 hansel and gretel got lost
2 jack and jill went up the hill
3 one day goldilocks went for a walk
4 father christmas is very kind
5 little red riding hood had a nasty shock in the woods
6 snow white was very pretty

UNIT 4 ● Writing

The accident

Report on my fall

One day I sat down on a wall. It was not very safe. I fell off with a bang and cracked my shell. All the king's horses and all the king's men came along. They tried to put me together again, but they could not do it. I don't know what will happen to me now.

Humpty Dumpty.

Write a report about an accident you have had.

Write:

1 where you were

2 what you were doing

3 what happened

4 how it ended.

Test 1   Do you remember?

● Comprehension ●

Samir was in his bedroom. His mum was cross with him. His bedroom was in a mess. There were books under his bed. His toys were all over the floor.

Answer 'true' *or* 'false' *in your book.*

1 Samir's mum was pleased with Samir.

2 Samir's bedroom was untidy.

3 Samir's toys were in his toy box.

4 Samir's books were under his bed.

● Using words ●

Write the animals' names in your book.

hamster   snake   lion   dog

1 _____   2 _____   3 _____   4 _____

In your book write an animal whose name ends in:

1 ___ at   2 ___ en   3 ___ ox   4 ___ uck

This rhyme is in the wrong order.

Write it in the correct order.

Do it in your best writing.

Put in all the capital letters and full stops.

when sam sneezed on wednesday she got a letter
when shiva sneezed on saturday she got lots of luck
when tom sneezed on monday he fell off a wall
when tamsin sneezed on thursday she felt better
when ben sneezed on friday he met a duck
when jemma sneezed on tuesday she lost her ball

Row, row, row your boat
Gently down the stream,
If you catch a jellyfish
Wave your arms and scream.

Row, row, row your boat
Gently round the lake,
Watch out for the crocodile
And look out for the snake.

Row, row, row your boat
Gently out to sea,
If you meet a big blue whale
Ask her home for tea.

'Row, row, row your boat' by Lucy Coats.

Write the answers to these questions in your book.

1 What should you do if you catch a jellyfish?

2 Where would you see a crocodile?

3 What should you look out for at the lake?

4 Who would you ask home for tea?

● Drip, drop, drip ●

The water from the tap goes

drip!

drop!

drip!

The flippers on the frog go

flip!

flop!

flap!

drip	flip	draw	flop	drag	flick
drink	flap	drop	flag	fly	drum

Draw a chart like this in your book.

Fill in the words from the box above.

'dr' words	'fl' words
drip	*flip*

Think of some more 'sn' words.

Write them in your book.

sniff!
sniff!
sneeze!

The ugly troll

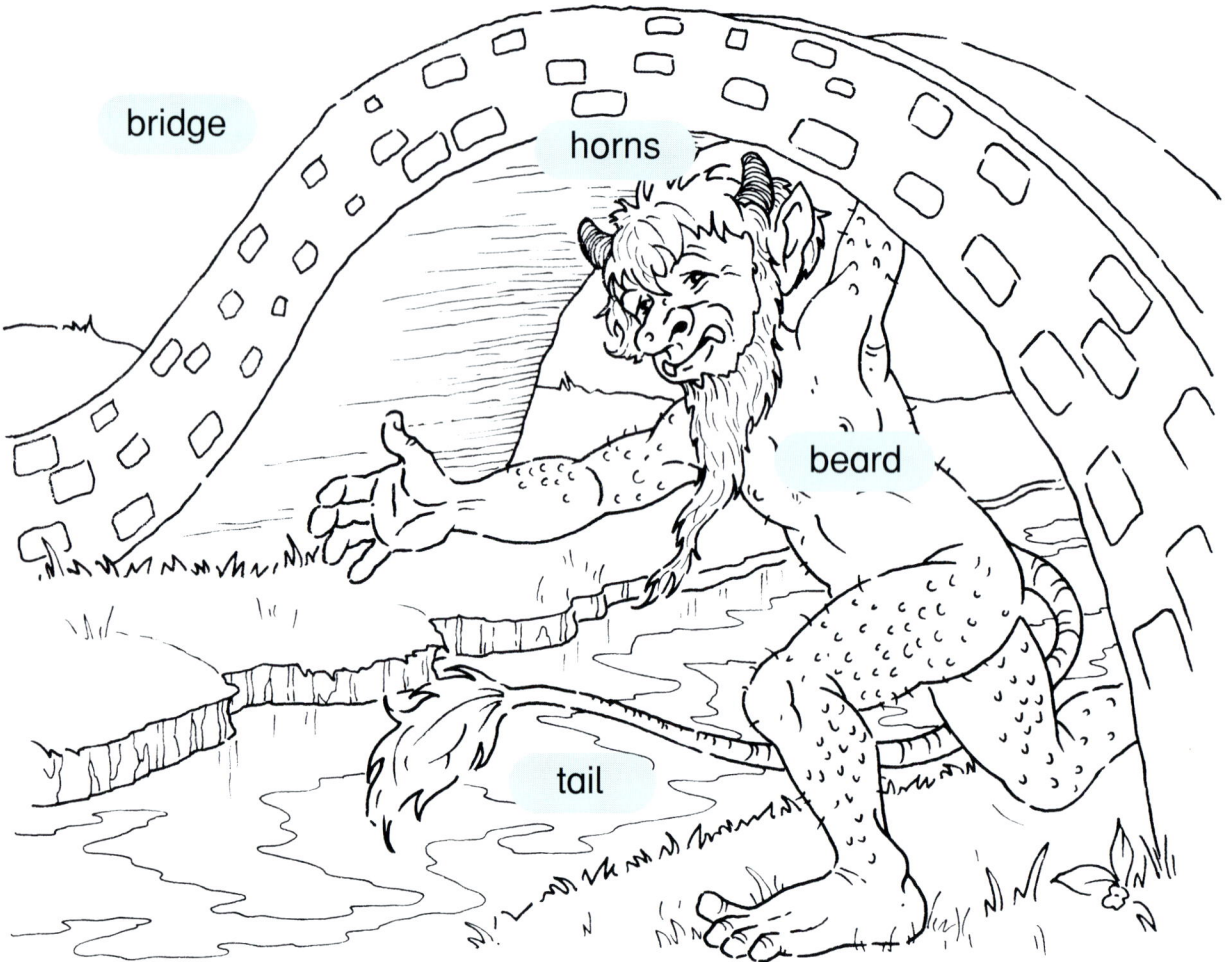

bridge

horns

beard

tail

Copy these sentences about the ugly troll.

Use some good words to finish them.

Put in capital letters and full stops.

1 the ugly troll lives under a _____

2 on his head he has two _____

3 he has a long _____ and a long _____

4 the troll is very _____

A walk by the river

Beginning

Ben and Sam went
for a walk by the river.

Middle

When they stepped on
the bridge an ugly troll
jumped out.

Ending

?

What happened next?

*Write an ending for the
story in your book.*

*Draw a picture to go with
your ending.*

*All stories should have a
good **beginning, middle**
and **ending**.*

Facts

● **Animal facts** ●

thick skin

large ears

short tail

big, heavy body

two tusks

trunk

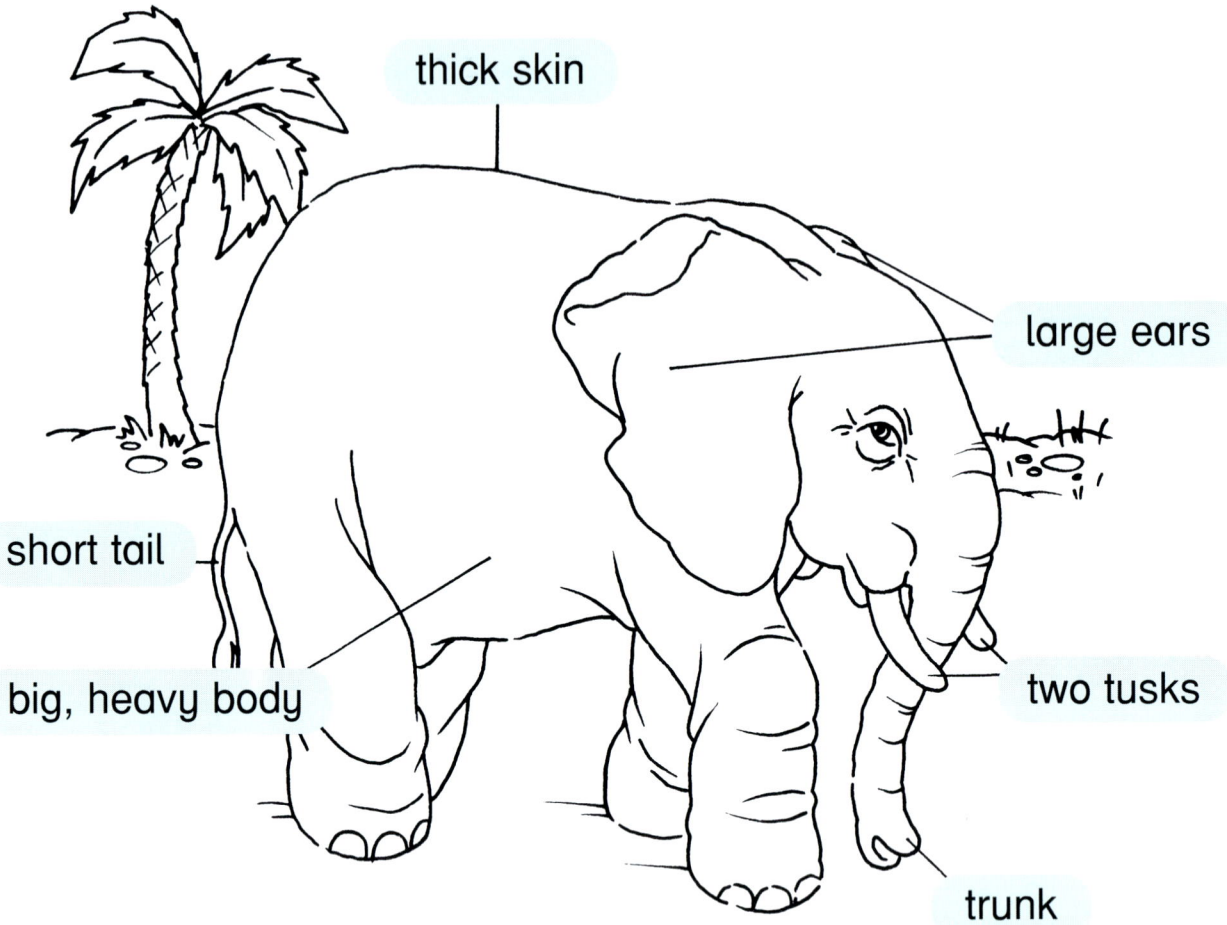

Write some facts about an elephant in your book.

*Write some facts about another animal.
Find a book about animals to help you.*

● Doing words ●

flaps   lifts   walks

'Doing' words are called **verbs**.

Copy these sentences about an elephant in your book.

Fill in the **'doing' words** in the gaps.

1 An elephant _____ slowly.

2 It _____ food into its mouth with its trunk.

3 Sometimes the elephant _____ its ears.

Now copy this rhyme into your book.

Use these **verbs** to fill in the gaps.

ran   jumped   laughed

Hey diddle diddle, the cat and the fiddle,

The cow _____ over the moon.

The little dog _____ to see such fun,

And the dish _____ away with the spoon.

● Questions ●

Copy this poem in your book using your best writing.

Put in the missing question marks at the end of each sentence.

How far are the stars
Why is grass green
How fast are cars
Would you like to meet a queen
Why is the sky blue
Where does it end
Why do horses have shoes
What makes rubber bend

Now write some answers to these questions in your book.

1 How old are you?

2 What colour is your hair?

3 Where do you live?

4 What do you want to be when you grow up?

*Write some questions for your friend.
Remember to use question marks.*

Writing directions

How would you get to the Ghost Train from the Fun Fair entrance?

Write and say which way to go.

Write what you would pass and see on the way.

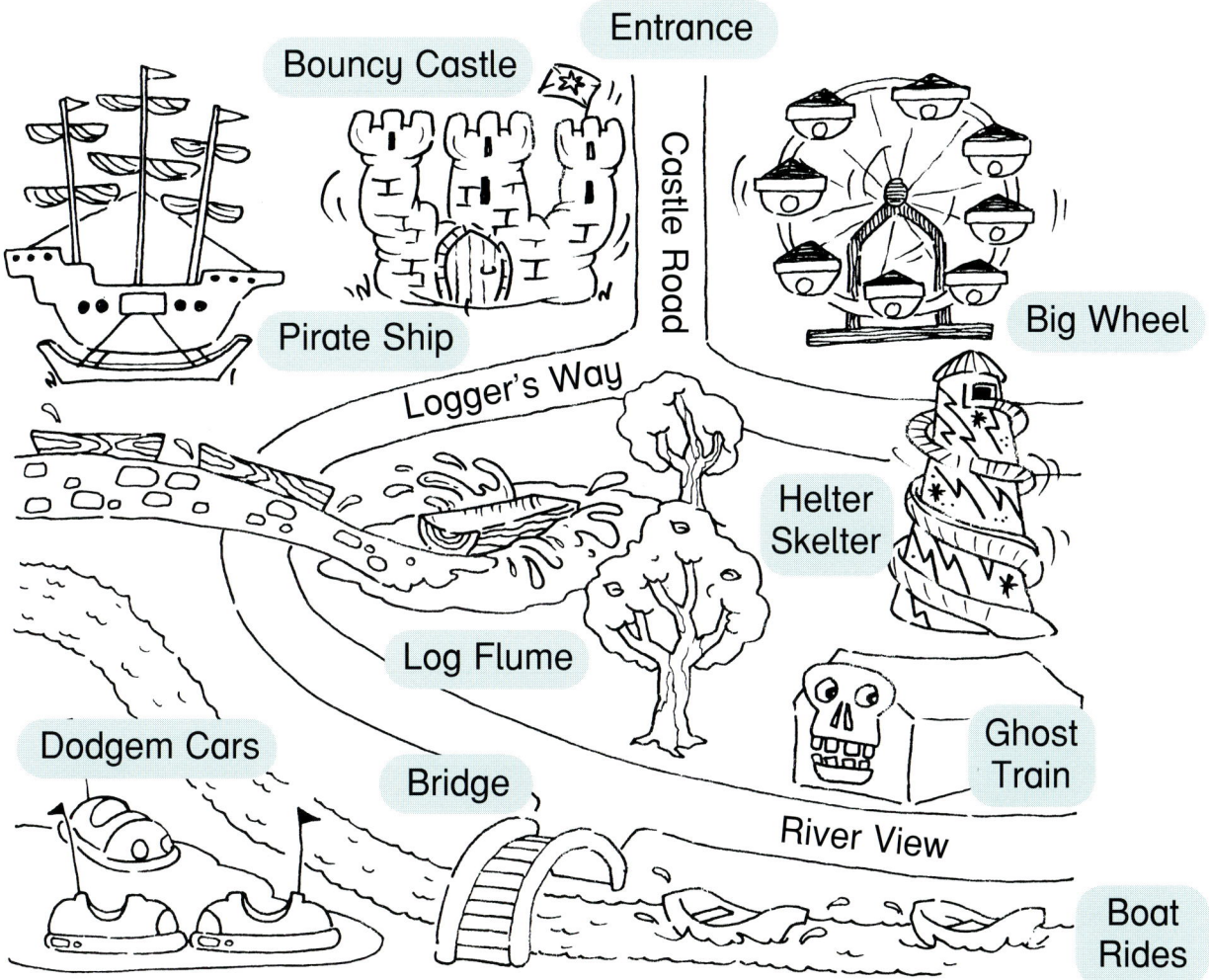

Entrance

Bouncy Castle

Pirate Ship

Castle Road

Big Wheel

Logger's Way

Helter Skelter

Log Flume

Dodgem Cars

Bridge

Ghost Train

River View

Boat Rides

Write and say how you get to school each day.
Which way do you come?
What do you pass?
What do you see?

● Becoming a frog ●

The frog lays her eggs.

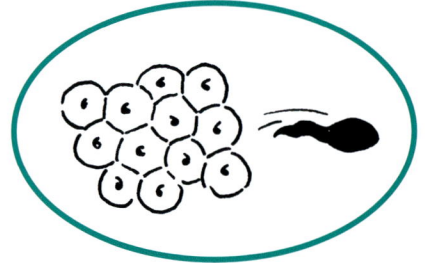

The tadpole turns
into a frog.

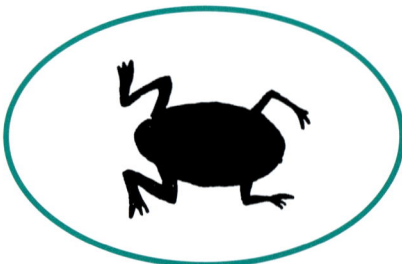

The tadpole comes
out of the egg.

The tadpole grows
two front legs.

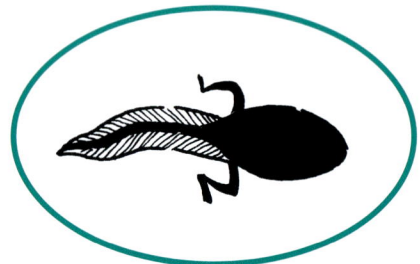

The tadpole grows
two back legs.

In your book write how a frog's egg changes into a frog.

● 'sh' and 'ch' words ●

Write the words in your book.

Finish them with 'ch' or 'sh'.

1

_ _ ip

2

_ _ ick

3

_ _ in

4

_ _ ell

5

_ _ op

6

_ _ ed

Change the first letters of these words to make some new words.

Write them in your book.

1 sh ip   Change the sh to r ⟶   *rip*

            Change the sh to t ⟶   ____

            Change the sh to sl ⟶   ____

            Change the sh to ch ⟶   ____

2 ch ick   Change the ch to k , p , fl , tr

3 ch in   Change the ch to w , d , sh , gr

4 sh op   Change the sh to p , dr , st , ch

Mixed-up sentences

Change these sentences so they make sense.

The first one has been done for you.

1 hop. Frogs can
  Frogs can hop.

2 is car The white.

3 children Most sweets. like

4 are black. Some cats

5 dog the The rabbit. chased

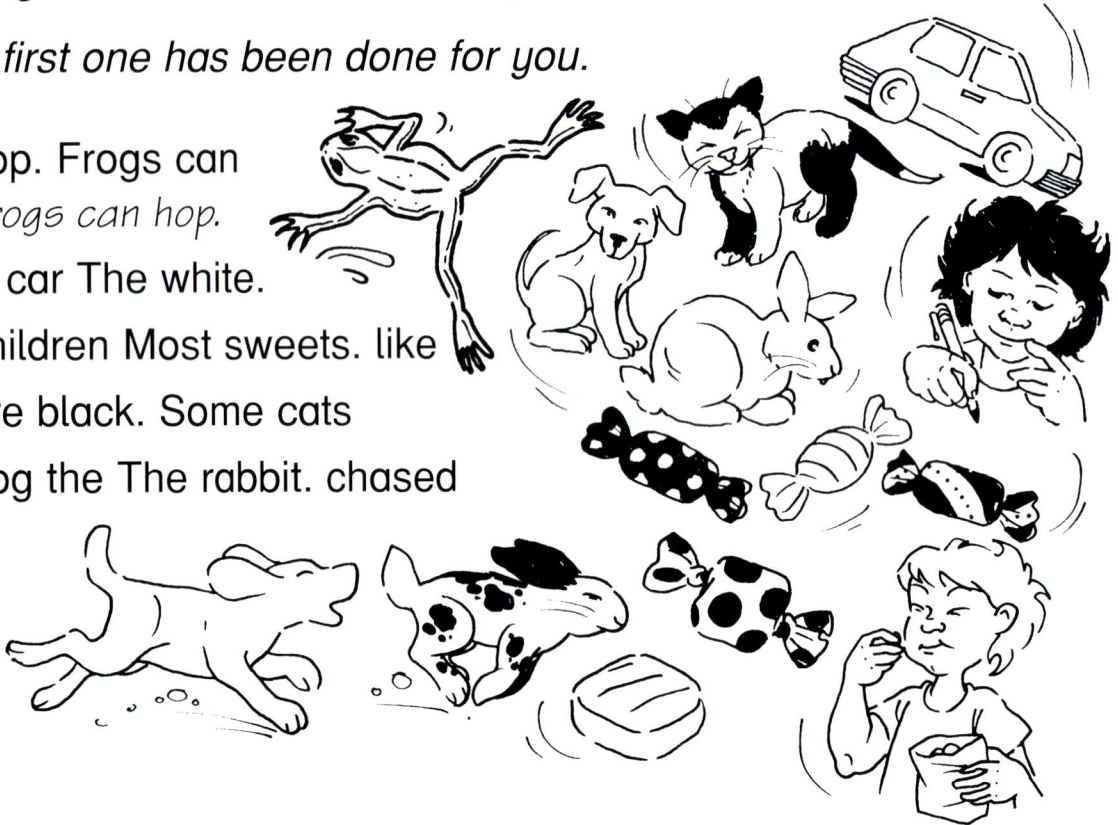

Decide which of these beginnings and endings go together.

Write the sentences you make in your book.

We dig	with a pencil.
We cut	with water.
We draw	with a spade.
We stick	with a knife.
We wash	with glue.

● Lost ●

LOST

A small kitten called Joey.
He has a white patch on his chest.
He has a collar with his name on.
Please let me know if you find him.

Reva Khan
14 Market Street

Imagine that you have lost a favourite toy.

Write a 'LOST' poster like the one above in your book.

Think carefully about what you need to write on it.

Ben Wood found my toy and gave it back.
Help me write a nice 'thank-you' letter to him.

Do you remember?

● Comprehension ●

In your book, write the part of the bike that each number stands for.

| bell | saddle | brakes | handlebars |

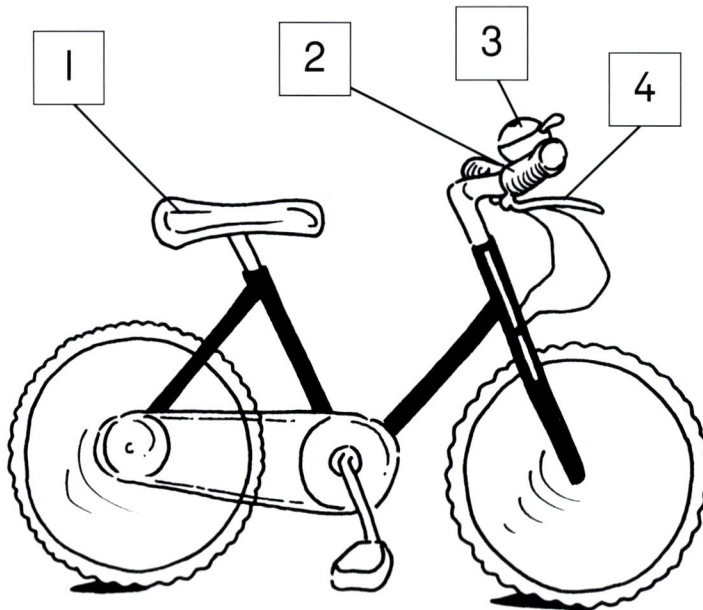

Write these sentences in your book and finish them.

1 You sit on the _____ .

2 You ring the _____ .

3 The _____ make you stop.

4 You hold the _____ .

● Using words ●

In your book write a word beginning with:

I ch _____ **2** sh _____ **3** fl _____ **4** dr _____

Copy these sentences. Fill in a sensible 'doing word' in each.

1 You _____ with a hammer.

2 You _____ with a knife.

3 You _____ from a cup.

4 You _____ with a pencil.

● Writing ●

Copy these sentences in your book.

Put in all the capital letters and full stops.

Write the sentences in the correct order.

have a wash

dry yourself

fill the bath with water

get out of the bath

take your clothes off

get in the bath

The king was very rich. He always got everything he wanted. One day he decided he wanted the moon. He told his servants to build a tower out of boxes. The tower was so tall it reached the clouds. The king climbed to the top of the tower. When he reached up to get the moon the tower wobbled. The king fell down with a crash. He did not try to reach the moon again!

Read these sentences.

Say if they are 'true' *or* 'false'.

Write the answers in your book.

1 The king was very rich.

2 The servants built a house.

3 The tower was made of boxes.

4 The king climbed into his bed.

5 When the tower wobbled the king fell down.

What do you think of the king?

● More 'doing' words ●

What is the king doing?

Write the answers in your book.

Remember, 'doing words' are called **verbs**.

The first one has been done for you.

| march | jump | bang | kick | paint | sniff |

1

The king is kicking.

2

3

4

5

6

Copy and finish these sentences correctly.

(sniff)

1 Yesterday the king *sniffed* a flower.

(bang)

2 Last week the king _____ his finger.

(jump)

3 Once the king _____ on his bed and broke it.

(kick)

4 When he was cross the king _____ the door.

(march)

5 The king _____ his men up the hill.

Questions and answers

a frog

a bird

a cat

a sheep

an elephant

Choose the correct answer to each question.

Write the answers in your book.

1 What has four legs, a tail and drinks milk?

2 What is green and hops?

3 What is big and grey and has a trunk?

4 What has two wings and a beak?

5 What has a coat made of wool?

Write some more questions about animals for a friend to answer. Remember to put a question mark at tne end of each question.

● Dirk – the dragon with no smoke! ●

Copy this story into your book.

Choose the best words from the boxes to finish the story.

	Once upon a ___time___ there was a dragon _____ Dirk. He lived on his own in a dark _____ . He was very sad.	called cave ~~time~~ cat
	Dirk looked just like other _____ . He had sharp teeth and _____ claws. He had a very _____ roar.	sharp dogs loud dragons
	But Dirk could not make _____ and fire come out of his _____ like other dragons. This made Dirk very _____ .	mouth unhappy house smoke
	All Dirk's friends made _____ of him. They called him _____ . Dirk just stayed in his cave all day and _____ .	names cried legs fun

> *Write a happy ending for my story in your book.*

● **The hedgehog** ●

The hedgehog comes out at night.
It eats snails and slugs.
The hedgehog has sharp spikes on its back.
If any animal tries to attack it, the hedgehog rolls into a ball.
The hedgehog makes its home from leaves and dry grass.
It sleeps all winter. This is called *hibernation*.

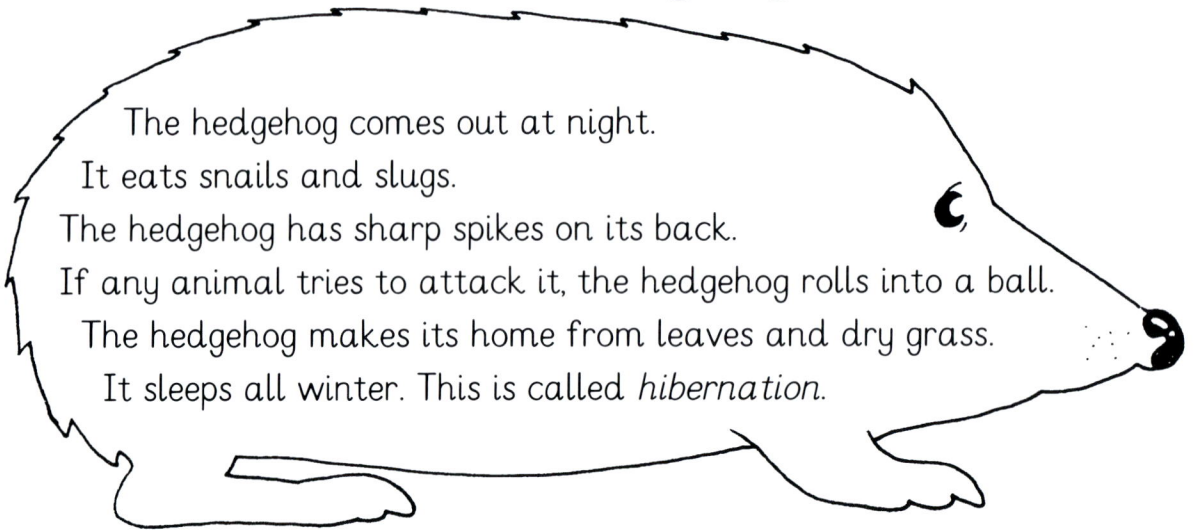

Choose the right answer for each question.

Write the answers in your book.

1 When does the hedgehog come out?

a) in the morning   **b)** in the afternoon   **c)** at night

2 Which of these things does it eat?

a) snails   **b)** cats   **c)** birds

3 What does the hedgehog have on its back?

a) a shell   **b)** spikes   **c)** horns

4 What does it do when it is attacked?

a) runs away   **b)** hides   **c)** rolls up into a ball

5 What does *hibernate* mean?

a) sleep all winter   **b)** go on holiday   **c)** eat things

● Looking for small words ●

Write the words.

Find the small words in them.

The first one has been done for you.

1 (hen)   w(hen)✗   t(hen)✗

2 (hat)   what   that   chat

3 (the)   then   they   there

4 (all)   wall   small   shall   falling

5 (ink)   pink   think   chink   sinking

6 (old)   sold   gold   golden   folded

Copy these sets of words in your book.

Write two more words for each set.

and	ill
band	will
grand	hill
panda	pills
handle	pillow

● Joining sentences ●

*Use the word '**and**' to join the pairs of sentences.*

The first one has been done for you.

1 The king fell down. The servants thought it was very funny.

The king fell down and his servants thought it was very funny.

2 I fell off the wall. I hurt my leg.

3 The boy saw the dog. He patted it on the back.

4 The bus stopped. An old lady got off.

Now join these sentences with 'but'.

5 The dog barked. There was nobody there.

6 Shirin is no good at spelling. She is very good at art.

7 The cat ran after the birds. They flew away.

● If I were ... ●

If I were a bear I'd grow long curly hair.

If I were a fox I'd wear stripey socks.

If I were a crocodile I'd run a mile.

If I were a dog I'd hop like a frog.

Make up your own 'If I were...' poem.

Use some of these animals in it.

mouse	cat	snail	hen	mole
snake	toad	sheep	seal	fish

● Tara's magic socks ●

One day Tara got a new pair of socks. They were lovely. They had different coloured stripes, just like a rainbow. Tara did not know that the socks were magic. When she put them on something strange happened. Tara suddenly started to fly! She flew up and up and up in the sky like a bird. She flew high above the clouds. When she looked down everything looked smaller — cars looked like beetles and people looked as small as ants! Her house looked like a little box.

Answer these questions in your book.

1 Who do you think gave Tara the socks?

2 What was special about the socks?

3 What happened when Tara put on the socks?

4 How do you think Tara felt when she put on the socks?

5 How did things look different when Tara looked down?

6 Write and say what you think Tara did next.

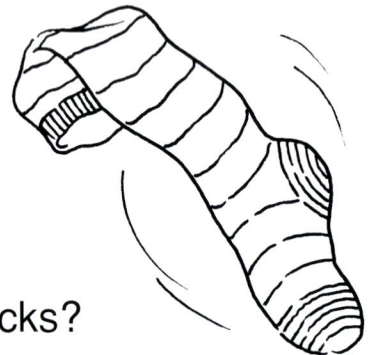

● 'Describing' words ●

Copy these words into your book. Tick the words which tell you about my socks.

old	new ✓	wet	tall
coloured	black	small	happy
bad	magic	lovely	flat

Describing words are called **adjectives**.

Copy these sentences.

Choose the best word to finish them.

1 An ice cream is → hot. → cold.

2 An ant is → big. → small.

3 Tara's socks were → new. → old.

4 A drink is → wet. → dry.

5 A mouse's tail is → short. → long.

6 A cake is → sweet. → sour.

A wizard's list

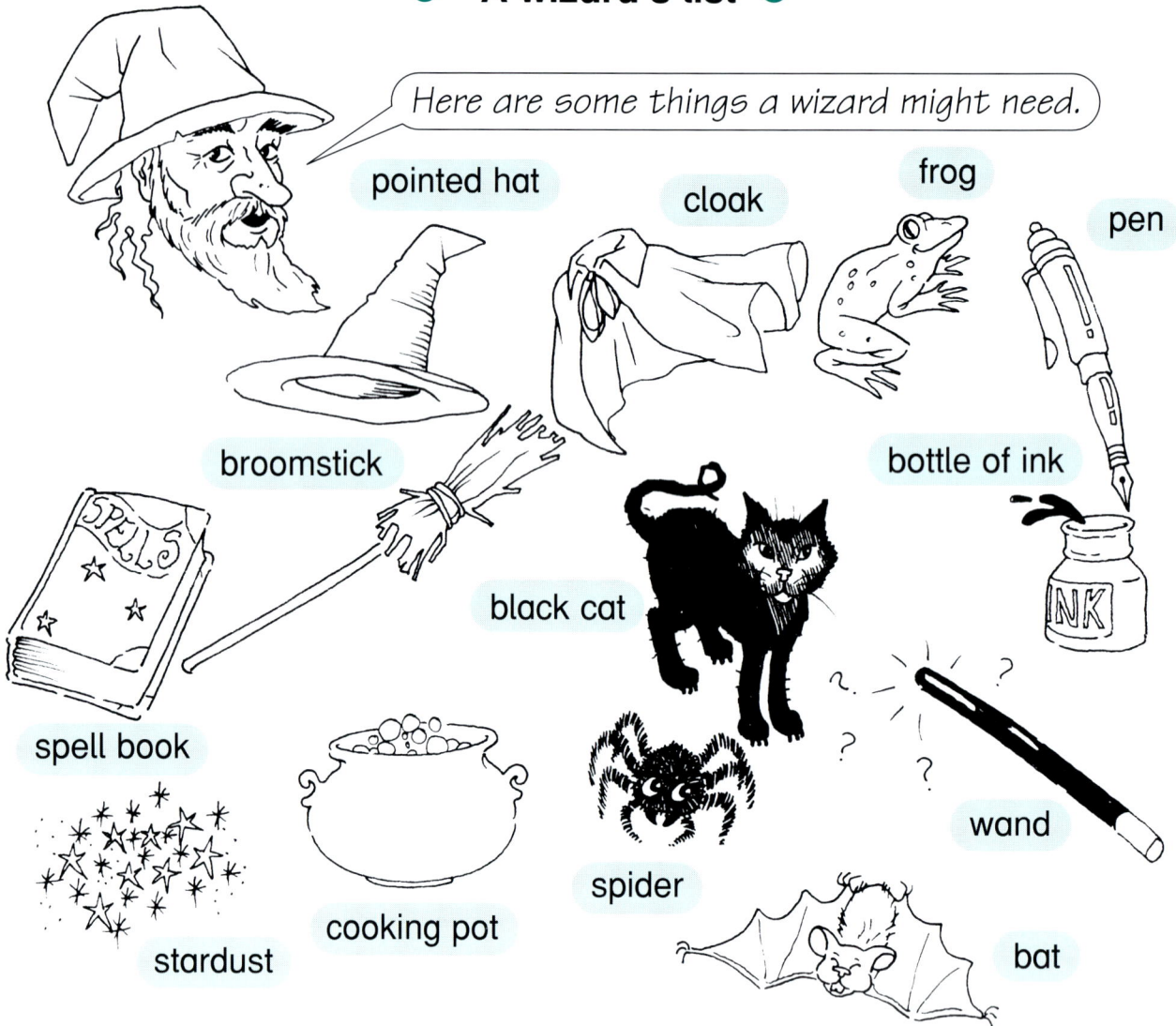

Here are some things a wizard might need.

pointed hat

cloak

frog

pen

broomstick

bottle of ink

spell book

black cat

stardust

cooking pot

spider

wand

bat

Choose eight things a wizard needs.

Write them as a list like this in your book:

What a wizard needs

a pointed hat

a

a

Things people say

In your book write ...

... something a wizard might say
when making a spell.

... something your teacher might say
when you have done some good work.

... something your mum might say
when your bedroom is too untidy.

... something you might say
if a dragon suddenly came into your classroom.

... something special you might say
to your best friend.

● **Comprehension** ●

Copy these questions in your book.

Put in all the capital letters and question marks.

Write the answers in your book.

1 is a red flag blue   **4** can a fish skate

2 is a cold drink hot   **5** does a banana have a skin

3 is water wet

● **Using words** ●

In your book write the name of something:

1 big   **2** hot   **3** short   **4** old   **5** wet

● **Writing** ●

Copy these sentences and put in all the capital letters and full stops.

Put them in the correct order to tell a story.

the branch broke   she climbed a tree

yasmin went to the park   yasmin fell down

she hurt her leg